# Harvest Year

by Cris Peterson

Photographs by Alvis Upitis

BOYDS MILLS PRESS

Honesdale, Pennsylvania

***Author's Note***

*American food production is a modern technological miracle. Most of the crops featured in this book grow in many states, and some of the crops were photographed in states other than those identified in the text. In most cases, the state identified in the text is a leading producer of the crop.*

Text copyright © 1996 by Cris Peterson
Photographs copyright © 1996 by Alvis Upitis

Boyds Mills Press, Inc.
815 Church Street
Honesdale, Pennsylvania 18431
Printed in China

Library of Congress Cataloging-in-Publication Data
Peterson, Cris.
Harvest year / by Cris Peterson; photographs by Alvis Upitis.—1st ed.
[32]p. : col. ill. ; cm.
Summary: A photographic essay about foods that are harvested year-round in the United States.
ISBN 978-1-56397-571-4 (hc)
ISBN 978-1-59078-783-0 (pb)
1. Agriculture—United States—Juvenile literature. 2. Food crops—United States—Juvenile literature.
[1. Agriculture—United States. 2. Food crops—United States.] I. Upitis, Alvis, ill. II. Title.
633 / .973—dc20     1996     CIP

Library of Congress Catalog Card Number 95-80775

First edition
First Boyds Mills Press paperback edition, 2010
Book designed by Amy Drinker, Aster Designs
The text of this book is set in 16-point New Century Schoolbook.

10 9 8 (hc)
10 9 8 7 6 5 4 3 2 1 (pb)

*To my father–in–law, Henry Peterson, whose help on the farm allows me to write.*

— C.P.

*For my mom, who could grow anything.*

— A.U.

Leafy lettuce in February...juicy melons in July...golden oats in August...barrels of cranberries in October.... Harvest is a year–round season in America. Every month food is produced in all our fifty states.

# January

When it's cold in the northern states, crunchy carrots are dug from the ground in Texas. Workers in Hawaii pick prickly pineapple by hand. Grapefruit as big as softballs hang on the citrus trees of sunny Florida, ready to be picked.

*Alexander squeezes the last drop of juice out of a grapefruit harvested from one of Florida's ninety-two million citrus trees.*

*Pineapples must grow
for twenty months
before they are ready to
be picked.*

*A Texas truckload of
carrots is ready to be
washed and bagged.*

*Harvesters walk behind the conveyor belt wings cutting each stalk of broccoli by hand.*

*During peak harvest, four million heads of lettuce— like the one Cody is holding— are picked daily in Arizona.*

# February

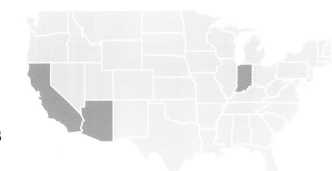

All year long, even in the cold of February, millions of chickens in Indiana lay eggs each day. Green bunches of California broccoli are loaded onto the "wings" of a machine that looks like a giant dragonfly. Arizona lettuce is picked by hand and trucked to grocery stores everywhere.

# March

As days grow warmer in March, syrup makers in Vermont drill small holes in maple trees to collect the sap for maple syrup. Hawaiian sugar cane is bulldozed into long piles and trucked to the sugar mill. Fresh, sweet milk from herds of cows on dairy farms in Pennsylvania is made into cheese, yogurt, and ice cream.

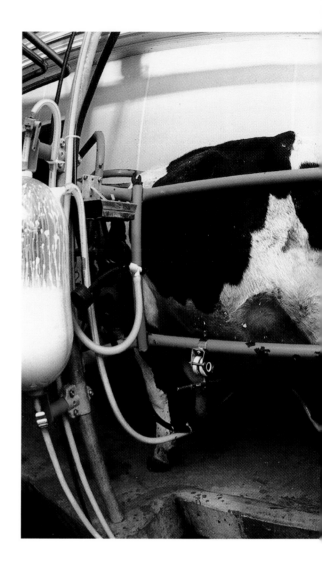

*Alex thinks raw cane is a sweet treat.*

*Sugar cane grows eighteen months before it is ready to harvest.*

Maarja tastes a spoonful of ice cream. There are over eight hundred million gallons of ice cream made each year in the United States.

Amber helps her grandpa milk cows twice a day in an automated parlor.

A maple tree must be fifty years old before it can be tapped. It takes forty gallons of sap to make one gallon of maple syrup.

Atlantic cod are often
frozen for fish sticks
and sandwiches.

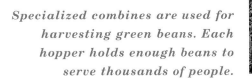

Specialized combines are used for
harvesting green beans. Each
hopper holds enough beans to
serve thousands of people.

# April

In April, warm sunshine ripens red strawberries in California. They are picked by hand and quickly shipped to all corners of the country. Atlantic cod are caught by Massachusetts fishermen on hooks and lines that are sometimes a mile long. Florida farmers harvest truckloads of green beans with mechanical pickers.

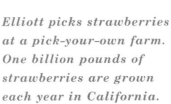

*Elliott picks strawberries at a pick-your-own farm. One billion pounds of strawberries are grown each year in California.*

*Onion bulbs grow partially above ground.*

# May

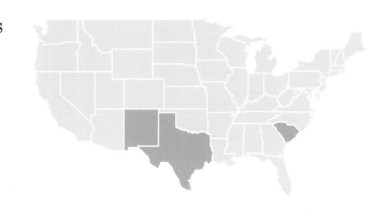

May is the harvest season for sweet onions in south Texas. They are picked by hand, loaded in burlap bags, and left in the field for a few days to cure. Melons from New Mexico are shipped across America in big boxes. Farmers in South Carolina handpick red, ripe tomatoes. One of them may end up topping your hamburger.

Whitney and Julia top off
their burgers with tomatoes.
There are twenty-one billion
pounds of tomatoes grown
each year in the United States.

Cantaloupe melons grow
on vines that measure up
to seven feet long.

# June

When summer begins in June, wheat is ready for harvest in Kansas. A big farm machine called a combine rolls across the field like an enormous house on wheels, cutting the ripe, whiskery grain. Fishing crews in Alaska net millions of salmon along the coast. Juicy Georgia peaches are gently picked by hand and packed in crates.

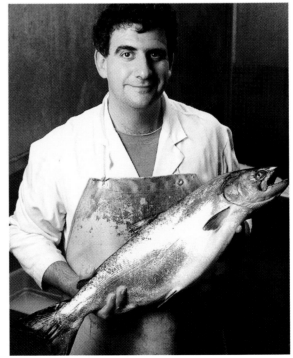

*Britta (above) loves fresh-picked peaches from Georgia, where over five hundred million peaches are grown each year.*

*This king salmon weighs ten pounds. Eight hundred million pounds of Alaskan salmon are caught each year.*

*Wheat, the world's most important grain crop, pours out of a combine.*

*Ripe wheat dances in the wind.*

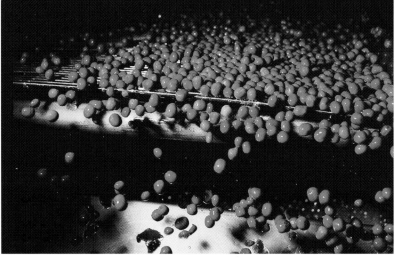

*Huge combines costing over a quarter million dollars harvest peas that are sorted and washed before freezing.*

# July

A mature cherry tree yields one hundred pounds of red tart cherries each year.

During the hot, sunny days of July, bright red fruit is shaken from the cherry trees in Michigan and made into juice, jelly, and other treats. Watermelons from Mississippi are trucked to stores, ready for picnics and seed–spitting contests. Green peas are picked in Minnesota and flash–frozen for year–round eating.

Watermelon is Ravi's favorite summer food. These melons usually weigh between five and forty pounds, but can be as big as one hundred pounds.

*Ravi, Chris, and Cody are shucking corn for dinner. Eight billion pounds of sweet corn are harvested each year in the United States.*

# August

Sweet corn, eaten fresh from the cob, is ripe in August. Ohio vegetable growers begin snapping the ears from the stalks in early morning so they have fresh corn to sell each day. Blueberries from Maine are hand-picked with special rakes and packed in crates, but they're especially delicious eaten right from the berry patch. In Iowa, oats are harvested with a combine and trucked to grain elevators.

*Whitney and Nick are handpicking wild blueberries.*

*Grain elevators that are one hundred feet tall store the oats. This oat field is ready for harvest.*

# September

As summer fades to autumn, apple orchards in Washington are ready for harvest. Eleven billion apples are handpicked each year in that state. Idaho potatoes are dug from the ground, washed, and packed into big bags for shipping. Beekeepers in North Dakota harvest honey by placing the honeycombs in a machine that spins around and forces the honey out.

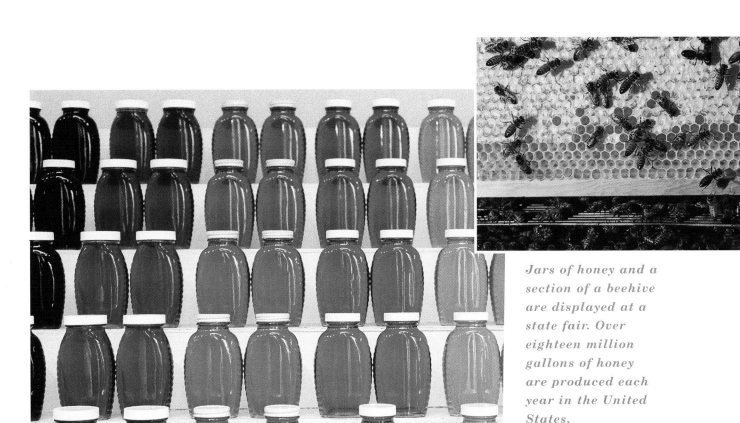

*Jars of honey and a section of a beehive are displayed at a state fair. Over eighteen million gallons of honey are produced each year in the United States.*

*B.J. juggles apples from one of Washington state's forty-five million apple trees.*

*Potatoes, the world's most widely grown vegetable, are loaded from the field.*

*Alexis and Tre love carving Halloween jack-o'-lanterns.*

# October

October is pumpkin time in many states, including Kentucky. Pumpkins are grown for jack–o'–lanterns and for pies. Farmers in Arkansas harvest rice with powerful combines and then truck the grain to mills where the hulls are removed. Cranberries from Wisconsin are harvested from flooded fields and floated to waiting conveyor belts.

Cranberry plants can produce fruit for one hundred years. The berries are guided onto a conveyor belt, then cleaned and loaded into trucks.

Eleanor is eating rice with chopsticks, as do millions of people throughout the world.

*Cartloads of grapes are weighed and packed into padded boxes. After cooling, they are shipped from the vineyard in refrigerated vans.*

*W.B. and Trevor love eating peanuts at the baseball game. Over one billion pounds of peanuts are grown each year in the United States.*

# November

November is the last month table grapes are gathered in California. Each bunch of grapes is carefully clipped by hand. In Oklahoma, peanuts are harvested with a peanut combine after the plants are dug from the ground. Turkeys from North Carolina are sent to market all year long, but many are eaten at Thanksgiving.

*These tom turkeys will weigh nearly thirty pounds at harvest.*

# December

In December, Louisiana fishing crews use trawl nets to harvest white shrimp in coastal waters. Pecan growers in New Mexico use mechanical shakers to shake the nuts from pecan trees. Thousands of nuts shower down from each tree onto a gathering tarp. Florida orange pickers with canvas bags slung over their shoulders climb tall ladders to reach the ripe fruit.

*Workers begin picking at the tops of orange trees and fill their bags with ninety pounds of fruit.*

Pouch-like nets called trawls are used to catch shrimp, which are quickly frozen on the boat to prevent spoilage.

Grandma's pecan pie is Natalie's favorite. Pecan orchards in the United States produce over two hundred million pounds of nuts each year.

Harvest riches from the land and sea are gathered in all year long. Using combines, conveyors, nets, hooks, and many working hands, farmers and fishermen produce the food that travels into stores and onto your table.

# FURTHER READING

***Eating the Alphabet*** by Lois Ehlert (Harcourt Brace).
A picture book that introduces fruits and vegetables, from apples to zucchini, to very young readers.

***Farming*** by Dennis B. Fradin (Children's Press).
A brief overview of farming from its history to harvest, illustrated with photos.

***Farming the Land: Modern Farmers and Their Machines*** by Jerry Bushey (Carolrhoda).
A photo–essay that follows farmers and their machines as they plant, cultivate, and harvest large sections of land.

***Food Resources*** by Robin Kerrod (Thomson Learning).
A brief synopsis of world agriculture illustrated with photos and maps appropriate for more advanced readers.

***Foods We Eat*** by various authors (Carolrhoda).
A series of photo–essays featuring facts about the cultivation, production, processing, and distribution of various foods.

***How Much is a Million?*** by David M. Schwartz; illustrated by Steven Kellogg (Mulberry).
A picture–book introduction to complex numbers that helps young children conceptualize huge quantities.

***I Want to Be a Farmer*** by Edith Kunhardt (Grosset & Dunlap).
A photo–essay that follows two preschoolers as they share a day on their family's diversified farm.

***If It Weren't for Farmers*** by Allan Fowler (Children's Press).
A photo–essay for beginning readers highlighting the work done on various farms and the assortment of foods produced there.

***Where Food Comes From*** by Dorothy Hinshaw Patent; photographs by William Muñoz (Holiday House).
A photo–essay emphasizing that all food comes from plants or the animals that eat plants.